I0446256

Side Hustle Starter Kit:

How to Earn Extra Money
and Create Multiple Income
Streams

Copyright Contents

All rights reserved. No part of this publication may be reproduced, distributed, or transmitted in any form or by any means, including photocopying, recording, or other electronic or mechanical methods, without the prior written permission of the publisher, except in the case of brief quotations embodied in critical reviews and certain other noncommercial uses permitted by copyright law.

Copyright © SIMON STERLING (2023).

Table of Content

Chapter 1: Introduction to Side Hustles

The notion of a "side hustle" has developed as a dynamic and revolutionary force in the modern landscape of work and money generation. It symbolizes more than simply an extra source of money; it signals a revolution in our perceptions of employment, security, and financial stability. In this chapter, we'll go on a trip to discover the essence of side hustles, their critical role in today's economy, and the inspiring experiences of people who have turned their side hustles into full-fledged enterprises.

The Definition of a Side Hustle

At its essence, a side hustle is an extra source of money sought in addition to one's principal employment. It is often motivated by passion, abilities, or interests that extend beyond the constraints of a traditional nine-to-five work. Freelancing, internet enterprises, consultancy, gig labor, and creative hobbies such as writing, painting, or crafts are all examples of side hustles. They may be short-term, seasonal, or long-term, and their variety is only limited by one's imagination.

The appeal of side hustles is their adaptability. They may serve as a creative outlet, a financial buffer, or a stepping stone to enterprise. Some people start side hustles out of need, while others are motivated by a desire for personal development, financial independence, or the opportunity to explore their hobbies. The draw of side hustles is their potential to grow into something far more than a supplemental revenue source.

The Value of Side Jobs in Today's Economy

Traditional concepts of job security and career pathways have transformed in a fast-changing global economy. The security that formerly came with a single, lifetime career at a single corporation is now a thing of the past. Because of the increase in automation, technical improvements, and economic uncertainty, people must diversify their income sources.

Side hustles have emerged as a viable reaction to these changes. They provide financial stability in an unpredictable world. Side hustlers may profit from various revenue sources, which function as a safety net during difficult times, rather than depending entirely on one salary. This flexibility is especially useful when unexpected events, such as economic recessions or global crises, interrupt conventional employment.

Furthermore, side hustles allow people to take charge of their financial lives. They give a platform for personal and professional development, enabling people to explore their interests and creativity. Aside from cash rewards, side hustles may help you improve your talents, develop your network, and raise your confidence.

In today's competitive work market, side hustle experience might help people stand out to prospective employers. It demonstrates a proactive, entrepreneurial attitude as well as the capacity to adapt to change, all of which are highly prized in contemporary organizations.

Success Stories: From Side Jobs to Full-Time Businesses

The potential of side hustles is arguably best shown by the countless success stories of people who took a simple concept and turned it into a profitable company. These triumphant stories demonstrate the almost endless possibilities of side hustles.

Brian Chesky, the co-founder and CEO of Airbnb, is one such success tale. Brian's side venture was Airbnb at the beginning. He and his roommates welcomed people into their San Francisco flat, offering a modest air mattress accommodation service. What started as a side hustle quickly evolved into a game-changing enterprise that altered the way people travel and experience hospitality. Brian's side venture eventually led to the formation of a multibillion-dollar corporation.

Another amazing trip is that of Mark Zuckerberg and his Harvard University buddies. Their side business, dubbed "The Facebook," was a little company aimed at uniting students on campus. Today, Facebook is one of the world's biggest social networking sites, and Mark Zuckerberg is a tech sector household name

These are not isolated incidents. Many company owners and entrepreneurs began with a side gig. They ventured to follow their hobbies or tackle issues that were important to them. These examples demonstrate the entrepreneurial potential concealed inside side hustles, demonstrating that with the appropriate combination of devotion, vision, and hard work, they may grow into big companies.

But side hustles aren't limited to the worlds of technology and entrepreneurship. Numerous people have successfully transformed their passions, talents, and abilities into lucrative enterprises. People are learning that their artistic hobbies may be commercialized, from making handmade cookies to selling handcrafted jewelry on Etsy.

In the next chapters, we will dig further into the realm of side hustles. We will look at how to identify your unique abilities and interests, make clear objectives, study lucrative ideas, efficiently manage your time, and build a long-term company strategy. Furthermore, we'll talk about marketing methods, financial management, expanding your side hustle, and overcoming obstacles on your path to side hustle success.

These experiences and insights will inspire and guide you as you begin on your side hustle adventure. They are proof of the transforming power of side hustles and the amazing achievements that can be accomplished when passion, dedication, and invention come together.

In the pages that follow, you'll learn about the tools and tactics you'll need to make your side hustle ideas a reality. Whether you are looking for financial stability, personal satisfaction, or the thrill of entrepreneurial achievement, this book will provide you with the information and motivation to write your own triumphant tale in the world of side hustles.

Chapter 2: Identifying Your Skills and Passions

Identifying your unique abilities, hobbies, and interests is likely one of the most essential elements in beginning a successful side business. This method has the potential to be revolutionary, resulting in a side hustle that not only increases your income but also meets your innermost aspirations and objectives. We'll take a deep dive into the art of self-discovery in this chapter, assisting you in unearthing hidden abilities, understanding your interests, and finally matching them with profitable side hustle options.

The First and Most Important Step is self-reflection

Before going on the thrilling path of discovering your abilities and interests, it's critical to pause for self-reflection. Consider the following inquiries:

What do I like doing in my spare time? Your inherent interests and passions are typically reflected in the activities you naturally gravitate toward.

What is it that causes me to lose track of time? Consider times when you are so involved in a task that hours slip by undetected. These are significant markers of activities in which you are interested.

What do people praise me for? Sometimes the abilities and qualities that come easily to you are the ones that others notice and value.

What were my childhood fantasies? Revisiting your childhood dreams might unearth secret passions that have been buried by life's duties.

What themes or topics do I find interesting to learn about? The topics that attract your attention often indicate your preferences.

What are the challenges that I naturally desire to solve? Consider the topics that irritate you and those you want to fix; you could discover a passion there.

Organizing Your Skills

After you've finished your self-reflection, it's time to map your talents. Skills are talents or proficiencies that you've acquired through time and may vary from technical to soft. Make a list of your abilities to begin. These may include:

Graphic design, coding, and video editing are examples of technical abilities.

Communication, leadership, and problem-solving abilities are examples of soft talents.

Cooking, gardening, and DIY home renovation are examples of practical talents.

Interpersonal abilities such as networking and connection development.

Knowledge or competence in a certain industry.

Take note of your degree of competence in each talent as you construct your list. Some abilities may be superb, but others may be primitive. This examination will assist you in determining areas where you can flourish in your side hustle ventures.

Exploring Your Interests

While skills are important, it is your hobbies and passions that will drive your side business. Your enthusiasm for a specific subject may be the impetus for the hard work and devotion necessary to achieve it. Consider the following measures to pursue your interests:

Make a list of your passions. Consider the topics, hobbies, or causes that really pique your interest. This might be a passion for classic vehicles, a love of animals, or a devotion to environmental protection.

Experiment with new things. Your interests may be lurking under the surface, waiting to be uncovered. Experiment with different hobbies, volunteer initiatives, or educational courses to find what appeals to you.

Seek out ideas from others. Read books, listen to podcasts, or interact with others who are enthusiastic about their hobbies. Their excitement may inspire you to pursue a new interest.

Consider what you would do for nothing. If you can think of anything you'd do for free, that's a good sign of your enthusiasm. It is sometimes said that when you like what you do, it does not feel like work.

Matching your skills and interests to side hustle opportunities

After you've determined your talents and interests, the next step is to match them with prospective side hustle possibilities. This entails searching for opportunities to use your abilities and pursue your interests. Here's how you do it:

Market Research: Look into the market to see where your abilities are in demand. For example, if you have a skill in web design, look for companies or people that need website development.

Exploration of Niche: Dive deep into your hobbies and look for niches that speak to you. If you're interested in health and wellbeing, look into side hustle options like fitness coaching, healthy meal planning, or wellness blogging.

Examine the point at which your talents and interests connect. Your side hustle is most likely to flourish at these intersections. If you have culinary abilities and a strong interest in sustainability, you may consider catering with an emphasis on locally produced and organic foods.

Considering Demand: Think about the demand for your proposed side business. Are there individuals or organizations prepared to compensate you for your talents and interests? To measure demand, do surveys, seek rivals, and examine internet forums or groups connected to your specialty.

Tips and Exercises for Discovering Hidden Talents

Discovering latent skills may be a thrilling voyage of self-discovery. Here are some exercises and pointers to get you started:

Journaling: Keep a diary in which you record your hobbies, your favorite activities, and any new skills you've learned. Journal reflection may show trends and interests.

Experiment with different talents and interests to find which ones appeal to you. This may be taking a painting lesson, learning to play a musical instrument, or dabbling in photography.

Seek comments: Ask friends, family, and coworkers for honest comments on your talents and qualities. Others may see skills in us that we fail to recognize.

Consider taking online courses that are relevant to your interests and talents. Websites like as Coursera, Udemy, and edX provide a diverse choice of courses that might assist you in exploring your strengths and hobbies.

Attend networking events, seminars, and workshops related to your areas of interest. Engaging with those who share your interests may give you with useful insights and chances.

In the following chapters, we will walk you through the steps of defining clear objectives, researching successful side hustle ideas, efficiently managing your time, developing a sound business strategy, and promoting your side hustle to the world. With your newly discovered abilities and interests as your basis, you're well on your way to creating a side hustle that not only pays well but also meets your greatest desires. Your side hustle adventure starts with this crucial stage of self-discovery, and as you go further, you'll find a plethora of options just waiting to be taken.

Chapter 3: Setting Clear Goals

Goals are the compass that guides your path in the realm of side hustles. They provide guidance, drive, and a feeling of purpose. Goals turn hazy dreams into practical strategies, turning your side business from a concept to a reality. This chapter is devoted to the art and science of defining clear, detailed, and attainable objectives for your side hustle, providing advice on creating a roadmap for your path and exhibiting real-world goal-setting examples to inspire and educate.

The Importance of Goal Setting

Goal setting is more than simply a regular activity; it is the foundation of your side hustle adventure. Setting clear objectives is the first step in earning additional money, pursuing your passion, or transitioning into a full-time entrepreneurial activity. Here's why it's important:

Clarity and Direction: Goals create a distinct feeling of direction. They assist you in determining where you want to go and what you want to accomplish with your side hustle.

Motivation is created when particular objectives are established. Goals motivate you to get up early, stay up late, and persevere in the face of adversity.

Accountability is enforced through goals. When you have specific goals in mind, you are more likely to take the measures required to reach them.

evaluating development: Goals serve as yardsticks for evaluating your development.

They allow you to monitor your progress and assess whether you're on the correct route.

Time Management: Setting objectives allows you to better manage your time and resources. You'll focus your attention on what matters.

The S.M.A.R.T. Goal Setting Framework

Consider the S.M.A.R.T. framework, which stands for Specific, Measurable, Achievable, Relevant, and Time-bound objectives. This framework guarantees that your objectives are clear and achievable.

Specific: Your purpose should be explicit and clear. Rather than just expressing, "I want to make more money," say, "I want to earn $5,000 per month from my side hustle."

Make your objective measurable. You may monitor your progress by using a specified measure. Here's an example: "I want to acquire 500 new customers for my online store in the next six months."

Achievable: Make sure your aim is both practical and achievable. Aiming high is important, but make sure it's within the range of possibilities. "I want to launch my e-commerce store in three months" may be more realistic than "I want to launch it tomorrow."

Relevant: Your aim should be in line with your ambitions and the purpose of your side business. It should be related to your overall objective. For example, if your side hustle is content development, "I want to publish a weekly blog post to grow my content marketing business" is appropriate.

Time-bound: Establish a deadline for your aim. A deadline instills urgency and keeps you on track. "I want to finish my first e-book in four months," offers you a specific deadline.

Making a Plan for Your Side Hustle

Now that you understand the significance of creating S.M.A.R.T. objectives, it's time to start planning your side business. A roadmap defines the major milestones, actions, and timeframes needed to achieve your objectives. Here's how to go about it:

Begin with the End Goal: Determine your ultimate aim. What do you want to achieve with your side hustle? This might be a specified amount of money, a specific number of customers, or the introduction of a product.

Break It Down: Once you've determined your ultimate objective, divide it into smaller, more doable phases. What are the checkpoints you must pass along the way? These may involve developing a website, establishing a consumer base, or initiating a marketing campaign.

Establish Deadlines: Each milestone should have its deadline. Be realistic, but maintain a feeling of urgency. A deadline holds you responsible.

Allocate Resources: Think about the resources you'll need for each milestone. This might include resources such as time, money, expertise, and tools. Make a strategy for getting these resources.

Prepare for Setbacks: Anticipate probable setbacks and problems. How will you deal with them? It is critical to have backup plans in place.

Make a graphic depiction of your journey's itinerary. A flowchart, a project management application, or a basic to-do list might be used. A visual plan may help you keep organized.

Goal Setting Examples for Side Hustles in the Real World

Let's look at some real-world instances of people who effectively established and accomplished side hustle goals:

Case Study 1: The Independent Writer

Jane loved to write, but she also had a full-time job in marketing. She established an S.M.A.R.T. goal of earning an extra $500 per month via freelancing. Finding her first customer, developing her writing abilities, and selling her services were all on her to-do list. Jane met her objective in six months by continuously presenting articles to numerous outlets.

Case Study 2: The Etsy Entrepreneur Michael was a creative person who specialized in handcrafted jewelry. He intended to convert his hobby into a side business. His S.M.A.R.T. objective was to earn $1,000 in monthly Etsy sales. His plan includes making a variety of jewelry, opening an internet shop, and promoting his wares. Michael accomplished and surpassed his objective after a year of hard work.

Third Case Study: The Digital Nomad

Sarah aspired to tour the globe while working remotely. Her ambition was to earn enough money from her internet consulting firm to support a nomadic existence. Her strategy included developing a portfolio, networking, and increasing her firm. Sarah now can work from anywhere in the world, thanks to two years of hard work.

These case studies show that goal setting is a fluid process that is not restricted by the scope of your ambitions. Setting clear objectives and building a roadmap may take you to the fulfillment of your aspirations, whether you're looking for a moderate boost in income or an ambitious lifestyle shift.

In the following chapters, we will go into greater detail about researching profitable side hustle ideas, effective time management, developing a comprehensive business plan, marketing strategies, financial management, scaling your side hustle, and overcoming the inevitable challenges that will arise. The goal-setting skills you learn in this chapter will act as a compass, leading you through the ups and downs of your side hustle adventure. Your side hustle adventure is unique to you, and with a well-thought-out strategy, you'll be well on your way to making it a resounding success.

Chapter 4: Researching Profitable Side Hustle Ideas

Share a variety of side hustle ideas across different industries.

Discuss market trends and the potential for growth in different niches.

Offer tools and resources for market research.

The world of side hustles is a wide panorama of potential spanning many businesses and niches. However, not all side hustle ideas are made equal, and starting your side hustle adventure with a well-researched concept may raise your chances of success dramatically. In this chapter, we'll look at a variety of side hustle ideas from various sectors, dig into the complexities of industry trends and development possibilities in distinct niches, and provide you with useful tools and resources for doing efficient market research. So, let us go off on an adventure of exploration and discovery.

Side Hustle Ideas from Various Industries

One of the most appealing aspects of side hustles is their adaptability. They may be adapted to your specific talents, hobbies, and market needs. Let's take a deeper look at some fascinating side hustle ideas from various industries:

1. Online shopping and e-commerce

Drop shipping: Collaborate with suppliers to sell their items online without carrying inventory.

Handmade Crafts: Make and sell handmade products on websites such as Etsy.

Print on Demand: Create unique shirts, mugs, and other items and have them printed and mailed on the spot.

Retail arbitrage is the practice of acquiring discounted or clearance products for resale at a profit on sites such as eBay and Amazon.

2. Design and the Creative Arts

Offer your design skills for logos, branding, and marketing materials as a freelance graphic designer.

Illustration & Art: Create one-of-a-kind artwork for customers, ranging from digital illustrations to conventional paintings.

Photography: Sell your photography prints or provide event and portrait photography services.

Web Design and Development: Create websites for companies and individuals.

3. Content Development and Writing

Blogging: Create a blog on a topic you're interested in and monetize it with adverts, affiliate marketing, or sponsored content.

Copywriting: Create convincing text for websites, advertising, and marketing materials for firms.

Social Media Management: Assist companies in managing their social media presence and expanding their online audience.

Create and edit videos for YouTube, social media, and business customers.

4. Consulting and mentoring

Business consulting: Provide experience in areas such as marketing, finance, or operations to assist organizations in improving and growing.

Individuals seeking personal and professional growth might benefit from life coaching.

Help job seekers with résumé writing, interview preparation, and career growth.

Nutrition and Fitness Coaching: Personalized coaching to help customers reach their health and fitness objectives.

5. Individual Services

Pet Sitting and Dog Walking: Provide care for dogs while their owners are away, as well as daily dog walking services.

Home arranging: Assist folks in arranging and decluttering their living areas.

Tutoring and teaching: Share your expertise by tutoring or teaching in topics where you excel.

Plan and arrange events ranging from birthday parties to weddings and business meetings.

6. Information Technology and Digital Services

App Development: Design mobile applications for your own company or customers.

Web development is the process of creating and maintaining websites for companies and people.

SEO and digital marketing are the processes of optimizing websites for search engines and managing online advertising campaigns.

Tech Support: Assist people or small companies with technology issues.

Property and real estate

Airbnb Hosting: Use Airbnb or other short-term rental services to rent out a spare room or home.

Property Management: Handles upkeep, leasing, and tenant relations on behalf of property owners.

Real Estate Photography: Focus on getting high-quality photographs of for-sale homes.

Market Trends and Growth Prospects

Choosing the correct side hustle concept entails taking into account market trends and prospective development in your selected industry. Here's how to assess the feasibility of a side hustle:

1. Recognizing Market Trends

Market trends give useful information about what is now in demand and where consumer preferences are headed. You may remain up to date by:

Examine Industry Reports: Many industries provide yearly or quarterly reports outlining industry trends and predictions.

Keep an eye on the news and publications: To keep updated, subscribe to industry-specific news portals and publications.

Participate in Online Communities: To evaluate the conversations and trends in your specialty, participate in forums, social media groups, and online communities.

Examine Competitors: Examine your possible competition to determine what works for them and where they may be lacking.

2. Evaluating Growth Potential

It is critical to evaluate the development potential of a side hustle concept to assess if it is a feasible long-term alternative. Take a look at the following:Research the size of your intended market. A larger market often provides greater potential for expansion.

Market Saturation: Determine the number of rivals in the market. To stand out in a crowded market, a unique selling proposition (USP) may be required.

Customer Demand: Conduct surveys, polls, or research to determine customer demand for your product or service.

Technological improvements: Think about how technological and industrial improvements may affect your specialization. Embracing new technology may be a growth driver.

Regulations and Barriers: Look into any legal or regulatory obstacles that may affect your side business. Compliance is essential for long-term success.

Market Research Tools and Resources

You may use the following tools and resources to perform extensive market research:

Google Trends: This free tool tracks the popularity of search phrases over time, revealing current trends and seasonal swings.

Google Keyword Planner: Use this tool to research popular keywords in your field. It might assist you in understanding what people are looking for on the internet.

Market Research Reports: Websites such as Statista, IBISWorld, and MarketResearch.com provide in-depth analyses of many sectors and marketplaces.

Social Media Insights: The majority of social media networks include analytics tools that give information on user demographics, interactions, and trends.

Questionnaires & surveys: Create surveys to acquire information from your target audience. SurveyMonkey and Google Forms make it simple to develop and distribute surveys.

Tools for Competitor Analysis: Tools such as SEMrush and Ahrefs may assist you in analyzing your rivals' online presence and strategy.

Industry-specific Forums and Communities: Participate in conversations, learn from others, and keep up to speed on trends by joining forums and communities relating to your area.

Professional organizations: Professional associations in many sectors offer tools, publications, and events to help you keep informed.

Real-Life Insight: Successful Side Hustles

Let us take a cue from those who have successfully transformed their side hustle ideas into profitable enterprises by finding market opportunities:

1. The Food Truck Phenomenon's Rise

The food truck market has grown significantly in recent years. Individuals with culinary expertise and a strong business spirit have taken advantage of the expanding trend of mobile food service. What began as a side venture for many food truck entrepreneurs has grown into a profitable company with a devoted following. Their success exemplifies how recognizing new trends and responding to customer preferences can lead to increased growth and profitability.

2. E-commerce Business Owners. The ease of online buying has fuelled exponential development in the e-commerce business in recent years. Entrepreneurs that recognized lucrative niches, sourced high-quality items, and built strong internet presences.

Chapter 5: The Art of Time Management

Balancing a side hustle with full-time work, family obligations, and other life obligations is a skill that might be the difference between success and exhaustion. Effective time management is essential for preserving homeostasis, completing objectives, and remaining sane during the process. In this chapter, we'll look at time management strategies to assist you in negotiating the challenging terrain of side hustles and everyday life. We'll provide you with tips on how to prioritize activities, keep organized, and maximize productivity. So, let us set out on a quest to perfect the art of time management.

The Difficulty of Juggling a Side Hustle with Other Responsibilities

When you start a side hustle while working full-time or juggling other obligations, you're simply adding another layer to your already hectic existence. This attempt requires a delicate balance and the prudent use of your most valuable resource: time. To be successful, you must handle a few basic issues:

Time Is Limited: The most apparent difficulty is a lack of time. There are only 24 hours in a day, and you must balance your side hustle with your job, family, and personal life.

Exhaustion and mental tiredness may result from juggling many duties. Managing your energy is just as important as managing your time.

Overcommitment: Taking on too much may lead to overcommitment, which can lead to burnout and a reduction in work and life quality.

Setting Priorities: It is critical to decide what to prioritize and what to delegate or delete. Not everything can be prioritized.

Techniques for Time Management for Side Hustlers

Effective time management does not need superhuman strength or a complex system. It entails identifying your objectives, establishing priorities, and determining the most efficient methods to spend your time. Here are some tips to assist side hustlers in retaining their balance:

1. Prioritization and goal setting

Set specific objectives for your side business and other duties before diving into the area of time management. Your objectives will act as a compass, directing your judgments on how to spend your time.

S.M.A.R.T. objectives: Set specified, quantifiable, attainable, relevant, and time-bound objectives for your side hustle as well as your full-time employment. This gives you a clear direction.

Prioritization entails distinguishing between urgent and significant jobs. Urgent jobs need immediate attention, but significant tasks help you achieve your long-term objectives. Concentrate on the latter while delegating or eliminating non-essential chores.

2. Scheduling and Time Blocking

Time blocking is a method of organizing your day by breaking it into different blocks of time allocated to certain tasks or activities. This strategy helps you to stay focused and avoid distractions.

Make a Schedule: Create a daily or weekly calendar that takes your full-time employment, side business, and personal life into consideration. Allocate precise time slots for each, and be consistent.

Batch comparable jobs: Combine comparable jobs to reduce context switching. Respond to emails, make phone calls, and attend meetings, for example, within designated time slots.

Multitasking should be limited since it might lead to lower productivity and increased stress.

During your time blocks, concentrate on one job at a time.

3. Time Management Apps and Tools

There are several tools and software available to assist you in properly managing your time. These digital assistants may aid you in streamlining activities and staying organized.

Calendar apps such as Google Calendar, Apple Calendar, and Outlook Calendar are great for scheduling and monitoring appointments, deadlines, and activities.

Todoist, Trello, and Asana are examples of task management apps that may help you build to-do lists, establish priorities, and manage work effectively.

Apps for Time Tracking: Apps like Toggl or RescueTime let you track how you spend your time and discover areas for improvement.

applications for Project Management: If your side hustle includes complicated tasks, applications such as Monday.com or Basecamp may help with project planning and task management.

4. Eisenhower's Matrix: Urgency vs. Importance

The Eisenhower Matrix is a useful tool for determining if a work is urgent, important, both, or neither. It's a simple four-quadrant matrix that might assist you in prioritizing your chores.

Urgent and Important (Quadrant I): These are activities that must be completed immediately, such as a job deadline or a client problem in your side hustle. Priority should be given to performing these activities first.

Important but not urgent (Quadrant II): These tasks contribute to your long-term objectives and should be scheduled. Skills development, strategic planning, and personal time are a few examples.

Urgent but Not Important (Quadrant III): These are jobs that seem urgent but add little to your objectives. When possible, delegate or reduce these responsibilities.

These jobs are neither urgent nor important (Quadrant IV). Remove or decrease them since they waste time and bring little benefit.

5. The Pomodoro Method: The Pomodoro Technique is a time management technique that promotes short bursts of intense work, generally

25 minutes, followed by a brief rest. This strategy aids in the maintenance of attention and the prevention of burnout.

Set a Timer: Pick a task, set a timer for 25 minutes, and work on it conscientiously. Take a 5-minute rest when the timer goes off.

Repeat: After four Pomodoro's, take a 15-30 minute rest. This pattern keeps you alert and productive all day.

Tips for Increasing Productivity

Various productivity methods may assist side hustlers in making the most of their limited time, in addition to time management techniques:

Establish clear boundaries between your side business, full-time employment, and personal life. To avoid burnout set defined working hours.

Delegate and Outsource: If possible, delegate work or outsource elements of your side business. This frees up time for other important tasks.

Procrastination is a time thief, so avoid it. Practice tactics such as the two-minute rule, which states that if a job takes less than two minutes, do it right away.

Use Artificial Deadlines Wisely: Artificial deadlines may generate a feeling of urgency, but they should be used sparingly. Do not hurry through projects to fulfill arbitrary deadlines.

Continuous Improvement: Evaluate your time management tactics regularly. What is effective now may not be effective tomorrow. Be adaptive and willing to improve your approaches.

Prioritize self-care, which includes getting enough sleep, eating well, exercising, and relaxing. A healthy body and mind are required for long-term productivity.

Real-World Insights: Time Management Success

Individuals' real-world experiences of effectively balancing side hustles with other responsibilities give useful insights into good time management. Let's look at some inspirational examples:

Case Study 1: The Working Parent Who Is Also a Blogger

Emily, a working mother of two, decided to establish a blog to follow her love for writing. Managing full-time work, children, and a side venture, on the other hand, was difficult. Emily used the following time management techniques:

Emily arranged her day, assigning distinct hours for her full-time employment, precious family time, and blogging.

Chapter 6: Creating a Business Plan

The path of a side hustle is a thrilling experience, whether you want to make additional money or convert it into a full-fledged company. However, like with any great journey, a chart is required to lead you through the twists and turns and to keep you on course when the seas get turbulent. Your company strategy is represented by that map. In this chapter, we'll examine the importance of a well-structured business plan for your side hustle, present you with a realistic template and instructions on how to develop one and go into financial forecasting and budgeting. So, let us begin the path of developing a road plan for the success of your side business.

The Value of a Well-Constructed Business Plan

A well-structured business plan is more than a paper; it serves as the basis for your side hustle. Here's why it's so important:

Vision Clarification: A company strategy might assist you in clarifying your vision. It compels you to consider your objectives, purpose, and how you plan to attain them.

Strategic Direction: It serves as a road map for your side business, laying out your plans and techniques. It assists you in establishing priorities and charting your course.

Risk Mitigation: A business strategy enables you to identify possible risks and difficulties and devise mitigation methods.

Investor Attraction: If you ever need finance or a partner, a well-written business plan may be a powerful tool for attracting investors and collaborators.

It assists you in allocating your resources efficiently, from time and money to talents and employees.

Measuring success: Key performance indicators (KPIs) in a company strategy enable you to assess your success and alter your tactics as required.

Accountability: It holds you responsible for achieving your goals and objectives. When you have a documented plan, you are more likely to follow through.

Making a Business Plan for Your Side Hustle

Now, let's go through how to create a business plan for your side hustle. It's important to realize that a business plan doesn't have to be extremely extensive or complicated, particularly for a side hustle. A well-structured, succinct strategy may be quite successful.

1. Executive Synopsis

The executive summary provides a high-level overview of the whole business strategy. While it is usually the opening part, it is generally simpler to write towards the end since it highlights the main aspects of your strategy.

Mission Statement: Describe the purpose of your side hustle and your goals.

Provide a brief description of your side hustle, including its goods or services, target audience, and unique value proposition.

Goals and Objectives: Summarize your main objectives and what you aim to achieve.

2. Company Description

This part delves into further information regarding your side hustle, presenting a complete picture of your endeavor.

Business concept: Describe your side hustle concept, its beginnings, and the issue or need it addresses.

Legal Structure: Determine if your company is a sole proprietorship, LLC, partnership, or other organization.

Market Analysis: Explain your target market's size, demographics, and trends. Determine your competition and how you want to differentiate yourself.

3. Goods and Services

Describe the items or services that your side business provides.

Product/Service Description: Describe what you're selling, including its features and advantages.

Pricing plan: Describe your pricing plan and how it relates to rivals' pricing strategies.

Unique Selling Proposition: Emphasize what distinguishes your goods or services.

4. Marketing and Sales Plan

This section discusses your customer acquisition and retention strategies.

Marketing Channels, Strategies, and Campaigns: Describe your marketing channels, strategies, and campaigns. This may involve social media marketing, content marketing, email marketing, and other methods.

Sales Strategy: Describe your sales strategy, including whether you intend to generate sales via Internet platforms, in-person sales, or other methods.

Customer Acquisition: Specify how you intend to recruit and keep customers, such as via customer relationship management (CRM) systems or loyalty programs.

5. Operational Strategy

This section discusses your side hustle's day-to-day operations.

place: Indicate whether your side hustle will be based at home, online, or a physical place.

Suppliers and Partnerships: Describe your supplier connections and any significant partnerships.

Production or Service Delivery: Describe how you intend to manufacture goods or provide services.

6. Financial Strategy

The financial strategy is an important element that covers the financial feasibility of your side business.

Startup Costs: Include the early costs of launching your side business, such as equipment, licensing, or inventory.

Provide financial predictions, including sales forecasts, revenue estimates, and break-even analyses.

Cash Requirements: If your side hustle needs cash, state the amount required as well as possible sources, such as personal savings, loans, or investors.

Budget: Present a budget that details your estimated monthly or yearly costs and revenue.

7. Management Group

Introduce the essential players in your side hustle, as well as their duties and responsibilities.

Your Role: Explain your position in the company, your credentials, and what you offer to the table.

Members of the team: Outline the responsibilities, abilities, and contributions of any additional team members.

8. Timeline and Milestones

Set clear targets and a schedule for the growth and development of your side business.

Short-term Milestones: Determine the accomplishments you want to attain in the next six months to a year.

Long-term Milestones: Identify other noteworthy achievements you want to achieve in the coming years.

Timeline: Include a timeline or Gantt chart to show when you expect to reach these goals.

9. Risk Evaluation

Determine the dangers and problems that your side business could encounter.

List possible dangers, such as market rivalry, financial limits, or external variables such as economic developments.

Risk Mitigation: Describe how you intend to minimize or handle these risks if they occur.

Budgeting and financial forecasting

Financial forecasting and budgeting are critical components of your company strategy. This section provides a clear picture of the financial health and sustainability of your side business. *Here's how to go about it:*

Estimate your predicted sales over a certain period, often the next three to five years. This forecast is based on your market analysis, pricing strategy, and sales strategy.

Expense Projections: Outline your projected expenditures, which may include salary, marketing charges, rent, utilities, and other fees. Divide your spending into two categories: fixed and variable costs.

Create a cash flow statement that monitors the movement of money into and out of your side venture. This statement can assist you in determining when you will have cash surpluses and when you may want more finances.

Break-Even Analysis: Figure out when your side hustle will become successful, commonly known as the break-even point. This study can help you determine how much you need to sell to pay your expenditures.

Budget: Create a thorough budget that accounts for all of your spending as well as your predicted revenue. A budget allows you to manage your expenses and remain on track.

Calculate the return on investment (ROI) for your side venture. This ratio calculates the financial return on your investment and assists you in determining the effectiveness of your side hustle.

Financial forecasts: Provide financial forecasts for your side hustle's first few years. Profit and loss statements, balance sheets, and cash flow statements should all be included.

Conduct a sensitivity analysis to determine how changes in critical factors, such as sales volume or costs, might affect your financial performance. This study will assist you in preparing for various circumstances.

Money Requirements: If your side hustle needs money, specify how much you'll need and when you'll need it. Explain how you propose to utilize the funding to help your company expand

Investor Presentation (if applicable): Create a convincing presentation that highlights your company strategy and financial predictions if you want to seek investors or finance. This presentation should give a compelling argument for investment.

Best Financial Management Practices

Consider the following basic practices to guarantee good money management for your side hustle:

Maintain Accurate Records of All Financial Transactions: Maintain complete records of all financial transactions, from sales and costs through invoices and receipts. Consider employing a professional accountant or utilizing accounting software

Maintain separate personal and business finances: Keep your side hustle's bank accounts and credit cards distinct. This split allows for more effective financial management and simplifies tax reporting.

Review Financial Statements regularly: Review your financial statements regularly to monitor the financial health of your firm. Determine where you can improve and change your methods appropriately.

Set Aside Emergency Funds: Set aside money for unforeseen costs or temporary income changes. Having a financial safety net brings comfort.

Put Wisely: As your side hustle earns money, put it back into the company to help it expand. Consider improving your equipment, extending your product range, or putting money into marketing.

Effectively Manage Cash Flow: Keep a careful watch on cash flow to guarantee you can fulfill your financial responsibilities. This involves timely bill payment, account receivable management, and inventory management optimization.

Taxes: Be aware of the tax ramifications of your side business and prepare appropriately. To maximize deductions, set aside a percentage of your earnings for tax payments and speak with a tax specialist.

Seek Professional Advice: If necessary, speak with financial counselors, accountants, or legal professionals. Their knowledge and experience may assist you in navigating difficult financial and legal issues.

Successful Business Plans in the Real World

Let's look at a few real-world instances of side hustlers who made detailed business plans and succeeded in obtaining insight into the efficacy of a well-structured business plan.

Case Study 1: The Entrepreneur in E-Commerce

John, a graphic designer who enjoys making personalized artwork, wanted to convert his hobby into an e-commerce venture. He started by developing a thorough business strategy that included:

Mission Statement: To provide one-of-a-kind, handmade art items that appeal to people looking for individualized home décor.

Industry study: John conducted an extensive study on the e-commerce art industry, identifying trends, competitors, and target demographics.

Marketing and sales plan: He devised a strategy that centered on harnessing social media marketing and engaging with home decor influencers.

Financial projections: For the first three years, John predicted his revenues and costs, preparing thorough income statements, balance sheets, and cash flow statements.

John was able to acquire a modest company loan using his well-structured business plan to cover early inventory and marketing initiatives. His e-commerce business blossomed, and by the end of the second year, he had surpassed his financial predictions.

Case Study No. 2: The Independent Content Creator

Emily, a full-time content writer, intended to start her freelance writing company as a side hustle. Her business strategy includes the following items:

Mission Statement: To help companies wishing to improve their internet presence with high-quality content development services.

Emily researched the content marketing sector, found possible customers, and evaluated the competitors in her field.

Marketing and Sales Strategy: She detailed her strategy to construct a professional website, produce a portfolio, and attract customers using social media and email marketing.

Emily forecasted her freelance revenue, allowing for several pricing techniques, and prepared a budget to manage her company expenditures.

Emily was able to progressively develop her customer base while continuing her full-time work thanks to a clear strategy. Her side business provided extra money, allowing her to ultimately shift to full-time freelancing.

Case Study 3: A Home-Based Catering Company

David, an ardent chef, wanted to put his talents into a home-based catering company. His business strategy includes the following items:

Mission Statement: To deliver delectable and customized food for private events and small groups.

Market Analysis: David investigated the local catering sector, identified target consumers, and assessed prospective clients' preferences.

To distinguish his firm, he intended to focus on word-of-mouth marketing, have a strong web presence, and provide distinctive menu selections.

David anticipated his revenue, taking into account seasonal changes and catering costs. He devised a budget to control the expenditures of first equipment purchases and meals.

David was able to get licenses, begin his firm, and gradually grow a customer base via referrals thanks to his well-structured strategy. His commitment to providing unique dining experiences paid off, and his home-based catering business thrived.

These case studies demonstrate how a well-crafted business plan may give direction, acquire finance, and assist side hustlers in reaching their objectives. A well-structured business plan may be a powerful tool for converting your side hustle into a successful endeavor, whether you're a creative entrepreneur, a freelance professional, or a gourmet aficionado.

Chapter 7: Marketing and Promotion Strategies

Marketing is the lifeblood of every company, even your side job. In this chapter, we'll go deep into the area of side hustle marketing and promotion tactics. We'll look at several online and offline marketing strategies, provide practical guidance on developing a marketing strategy, and share inspirational case studies of great side hustlers and the marketing strategies that helped them succeed.

The Influence of Effective Marketing

Marketing is the art of engaging with your target audience, determining their requirements, and offering a solution. Effective marketing may help you accomplish many essential goals in the context of your side hustle:

Marketing may help you raise knowledge about your side hustle, ensuring that prospective buyers are aware that your items or services exist.

Acquisition: It makes it easier to acquire new consumers or clients, so growing your reach and impact.

Retention: Marketing allows you to keep in touch with your current clients, promoting repeat business and loyalty

Marketing is a driver for corporate development and expansion by reaching a larger audience and interacting successfully.

Competitive Advantage: Strategic marketing distinguishes you from the competition by emphasizing your unique value offer.

Making a Marketing Strategy

A well-crafted marketing plan is the foundation of a successful marketing strategy. Here's a step-by-step tutorial on making one for your side business:

1. Recognize Your Target Audience:

Before you can properly promote your side hustle, you must first identify your target consumer. Take into account demographics, hobbies, pain spots, and habits. Making client personas may assist with this approach.

2. Establish Your Value Proposition:

What distinguishes your side hustle? What makes your product or service superior to others? Define your value proposition clearly, since it will serve as the foundation of your marketing activities.

3. Set specific objectives:

Your marketing strategy should be in line with your entire company's objectives. Define clear, quantifiable goals that you wish to attain, such as meeting a sales target, boosting website traffic, or building your social media following.

4. Select the Best Marketing Channels:

Choose the most effective marketing channels for reaching your target demographic. Social media, email marketing, content marketing, search engine optimization (SEO), and pay-per-click advertising are examples of online channels. Events, print advertising, and direct mail are examples of offline methods.

5. Create a Content Strategy:

In today's digital age, content reigns supreme. Create a content plan that includes blog entries, social media updates, videos, and other sorts of material that are appealing to your target audience. Content should be educational, entertaining, and useful.

6. Make a Budget:

Determine how much money you can devote to marketing. The breadth and extent of your marketing initiatives will be determined by your budget.

7. Campaigns and initiatives should be planned:

Create campaigns or initiatives to organize your marketing efforts. Each campaign should have a specific goal, timetable, and money. For instance, you may run a campaign to promote a new product or a social media campaign to raise brand recognition.

8. Implement and carry out:

Once you've established your strategy, it's time to put it into action. Begin by developing content, running advertisements, connecting with your audience, and tracking your success.

9. Measure and monitor:

Track the success of your marketing campaigns on a regular basis. To assess the efficacy of your efforts, use analytics and key performance indicators (KPIs).

10. Adjust and improve:

Make changes to your marketing strategy based on the data and insights you collect. Optimize your tactics to obtain better outcomes and more efficiently.

Strategies for Online Marketing

Online marketing is a valuable tool for side hustlers since it enables you to access a worldwide audience and communicate with prospective consumers at all hours of the day and night. Consider the following excellent web marketing strategies:

1. Marketing on Social Media:

Connect with your audience by using social media sites such as Facebook, Instagram, Twitter, LinkedIn, and Pinterest. Create a content schedule, publish interesting pieces, and think about executing paid advertising campaigns to attract a larger following.

2. Marketing using Content:

Blogging, video content, and other kinds of content marketing may help you position yourself as an expert in your industry and drive organic traffic to your website. Concentrate on creating useful and helpful content that addresses your audience's problem points.

3. Email Promotion:

Creating an email list is a great resource. Send your subscribers frequent mailings, incentives, and updates. For more focused marketing, use automation to tailor content and segment your email list.

4. SEO (Search Engine Optimization)

Improve your organic (non-paid) presence by optimizing your website for search engines. Research relevant keywords, generate high-quality content, and optimize the technical components of your website.

5. PPC (Pay-Per-Click) Marketing:

Paid advertising, such as Google Ads or Facebook Ads, may assist you in reaching a targeted audience rapidly. Set a budget, identify your target demographic, and develop interesting advertising campaigns.

6. Affiliate Promotion:

Consider collaborating with affiliates or influencers in your field who may advertise your goods or services to their audiences in return for a sales fee.

7. Marketplaces on the internet:

Consider selling on internet markets such as Etsy, Amazon, or eBay if suitable for your side business. These platforms have built-in audiences and may help you reach a wider audience.

Strategies for Offline Marketing

While internet marketing is important for many side hustles, don't overlook the effectiveness of offline marketing methods, particularly if your target audience is local or has a physical presence. Consider the following offline marketing strategies:

1. Networking:

Participate in local business events, conferences, and meetings to meet new clients, collaborators, and partners.

2. Flyers and business cards:

Create excellent business cards and flyers to hand out at local events, on neighborhood bulletin boards, or by direct mail.

3. Local Marketing:

To target a local audience, consider advertising in local newspapers, magazines, or radio stations.

4. Attending Trade Shows & Exhibitions:

Participating in trade events or exhibits, if applicable to your side hustle, may help you display your goods or services to a bigger audience.

5. Organizing Workshops or Seminars

Consider providing instructional classes or events relating to your side venture. This establishes you as an authority in your industry and enables you to meet with possible consumers in person.

6. Collaborations & Partnerships:

Investigate collaborations with local firms that compliment your goods or services. For example, if you make personalized candles, consider partnering with a local spa to market your wares.

Case Studies: *Successful Entrepreneurs and Their Marketing Strategies*

To demonstrate the potential of successful marketing methods for side hustlers, consider case studies of people who converted their side hustles into profitable enterprises by combining online and offline marketing strategies.

Case Study 1: The Artisan of Handmade Jewelry

Meet Sarah, a jewelry artist who started her side career by creating one-of-a-kind handcrafted jewelry. Sarah's marketing strategy comprised the following elements:

Sarah built an online presence by developing a professional website and establishing social media accounts on Instagram and Facebook. She utilized these media to promote her jewelry and communicate with her fans.

Sarah launched a blog on her website to give insights into her creative process, jewelry maintenance recommendations, and style guidelines. Her blog not only drew organic visitors but also established her as an industry authority.

Sarah urged visitors to her website to subscribe to her newsletter in order to establish a loyal consumer base. She sends out frequent emails with information about new collections, promotions, and the tales behind her designs.

Sarah engaged her social media followers by replying to comments, holding contests, and cooperating with micro-influencers who shared her love for handcrafted jewelry.

Local Craft Fairs: While Sarah's primary business was online, she also attended local craft fairs and artisan markets. These events enabled her to interact with her local audience and raise brand awareness.

Sarah's side business increased significantly as she dedicated herself to both online and offline marketing. She grew her jewelry line, recruited more assistants, and finally became a full-time jewelry designer. Her marketing methods were critical to her success.

Case Study No. 2: The Independent Graphic Designer

John, a full-time freelance graphic designer, sought to turn his freelancing business into a profitable side income. His marketing strategy includes the following elements:

Portfolio Website: John designed a professional portfolio website to display his design work. A clean and straightforward portfolio of his work, customer testimonials, and a blog where he provided design suggestions and industry insights were all included on his website.

Social Media Promotion: To showcase his design work and communicate with prospective customers, John used social media sites, notably Instagram and LinkedIn. To broaden his network, he utilized certain hashtags and joined design-related LinkedIn groups.

Email Marketing: John gathered email addresses from prospective customers who visited his website or indicated an interest in his services. He sent out monthly emails to subscribers that contained design suggestions, industry news, and unique deals.

Despite working full-time, John made an effort to attend local networking events and industry conferences. This enabled him to network with possible customers and other specialists in the sector.

Freelancing Platforms: To obtain short-term assignments and acquire exposure to a worldwide customer base, John joined freelancing platforms such as Upwork and Fiverr.

John's side business thrived as a result of a strong online presence, social media involvement, and a devotion to networking. He was able to acquire long-term contracts, allowing him to finally convert to full-time freelancing.

Personal Chef and Caterer Case Study 3

David, an enthusiastic home cook, wanted to supplement his income as a personal chef and caterer. His marketing strategy includes the following elements:

Local SEO: David optimized his website for local search, ensuring that when prospective clients looked for catering services in his region, it appeared in local search results.

David executed sponsored social media advertising efforts to reach out to local audiences. These commercials highlighted his culinary skills and provided unique advertising for local events.

Engaging Local companies: David approached local companies, event planners, and venues to form alliances and provide his food services. He often attended local business meetings and events to network.

David conducted sampling events where participants may try his meals to offer prospective consumers a firsthand experience of his culinary expertise. These events were promoted both online and through local networks.

Word of Mouth: David encouraged happy clients to tell others about his catering services. Clients who recommended new businesses received referral bonuses from him.

David's one-of-a-kind blend of internet marketing efforts, focused local initiatives, and great culinary offerings enabled his side business to prosper. His reputation as a personal chef and caterer grew as he got continuous bookings for weddings, business events, and private parties.

These case studies show the many marketing strategies that might lead to success in the realm of side hustles. Effective marketing may help you transform your side hustle into a profitable company, whether you're making handcrafted jewelry, delivering freelance services, or providing culinary delights.

Measuring the ROI of Your Marketing Strategies

You'll need to use a variety of metrics and key performance indicators (KPIs) to measure the efficacy of your marketing strategy. These indicators will assist you in determining if your efforts are producing the expected outcomes and will give insights into where you can improve.

1. Monitor the amount of visitors to your website and how they found it, whether via search engines, social media, or other means.

2. Conversion Rate: Calculate the proportion of website visitors who complete a desired activity, such as completing a purchase, signing up for a newsletter, or seeking more information.

3. Click-Through Rate (CTR): Measure the proportion of individuals who click on your ad after viewing it to evaluate the success of your online ads.

4. Social Media Involvement: Examine the level of involvement on your social media postings, such as the number of likes, comments, shares, and followers obtained.

5. **Track KPIs** like as open rates, click-through rates, and conversion rates for your email marketing campaigns.

6. **Sales and revenue** growth should be tracked to see whether your marketing initiatives are having a beneficial influence on your bottom line.

7. **client Acquisition Cost (CAC):** Determine how much it will cost to acquire each new client via your marketing activities. This indicator assists you in determining the effectiveness of your marketing budget.

8. **Return on Investment (ROI):** Calculate the ROI of your marketing activities. This metric will show how much money you produce for every dollar spent on marketing.

9. Customer Retention Rate: The proportion of customers who continue to conduct business with you after a certain amount of time. A high percentage of client retention indicates good marketing and consumer satisfaction.

10. Survey and Feedback: Use surveys, reviews, and direct contact to get feedback from your consumers and target audience. This qualitative data might shed light on the success of your marketing activities.

It is critical to analyze these numbers on a regular basis and adapt your marketing efforts appropriately. Experiment with diverse tactics, explore new ideas and react to changes in the preferences of your target audience. Your marketing strategy should vary over time to reflect what works best for your side business.

Last Thoughts

Marketing and marketing are critical components of the success of your side business. A well-thought-out marketing strategy may help you reach your target audience, attract consumers, and develop your company, whether you're operating in the internet world or connecting with your local community. Experiment, fine-tune your tactics, and adapt to the ever-changing marketing scene. With the correct marketing strategy, you can take your side hustle to the next level and turn it into a full-fledged company.

Chapter 8: Managing Finances and Taxes

Running a side hustle may be a fun and financially rewarding enterprise, but the financial elements must be handled with caution and wisdom. In this chapter, we'll dive into the area of handling money and taxes for your side business, giving you tips on how to properly manage revenue, costs, and tax duties. We'll also discuss tax breaks and offer crucial financial best practices to safeguard your side hustle's financial health.

The Financial Aspects of Having a Second Job

Whether your side hustle is motivated by a passion, a need for additional cash, or a desire to test a company concept, effective financial management is critical to its success. Let's begin with the core financial factors of your side hustle:

1. Income: All money earned from your side business, whether via sales, services, or any other means. It is your company's lifeblood and a key source of profit.

2. Expenses: These are the charges of operating your side business. They include anything from product prices and marketing charges to the procurement of equipment and software.

3. Profit: The amount left over after subtracting costs from your revenue is your profit. It is the monetary reward for your efforts and a crucial measure of your company's success.

4. Cash Flow: The movement of money into and out of your firm is referred to as cash flow.

Managing cash flow is critical for paying bills, investing in development, and guaranteeing your side hustle's financial stability.

5. Taxes: Taxes are an important component of your financial obligations. You must declare and pay taxes on your side hustle earnings. Income tax, self-employment tax, and potentially additional municipal or state taxes are included.

Advice on Managing Your Income and Expenses

Effective revenue and spending control are the foundation of your side hustle's financial success. Here are some key tips to remember:

1. Income Tracking:

Set up a dependable strategy for tracking your side hustle earnings. Consider bookkeeping software or a basic spreadsheet.

Ensure that all sources of money, whether from product sales, services, or other revenue streams, are reported.

Keep precise records of all payments, including the date, source, and amount.

2. Expense Management:

For your side venture, have a separate bank account and credit card. This split makes tracking and managing spending simpler.

To determine where your money is going, categorize your costs, such as marketing, office supplies, or equipment.

All costs should be documented with receipts and invoices. This paperwork is essential for tax breaks and financial planning.

3. Creating a budget:

Make a budget for your side venture that details predicted revenue and costs.

Review and change your budget regularly depending on real income and expenditure.

4. Set a Price for Your Products or Services:

Set rates that cover your expenditures while also allowing for a profit margin. Never undervalue your efforts or your goods.

When pricing your products, keep the competition and market demand in mind.

5. Investing and Saving:

Set aside some of your earnings for savings or investment in your side business. This may be utilized for growth, marketing, or emergencies.

Consider establishing a separate savings account for your company's finances.

Perspectives on Tax Responsibilities

Taxes are an important part of managing the finances of your side business. Here's a rundown of your main tax obligations:

1. Tax on Self-Employment:

If you make money through a side hustle, you must normally pay self-employment tax. This tax includes payments to Social Security and Medicare. It is essential to calculate and put away a part of your earnings for self-employment tax.

2. Personal Income Tax:

Your side hustle revenue, like any other, is subject to income tax. When you submit your yearly tax return, you must record your earnings and pay income tax on your side hustle revenue.

3. Estimated Quarterly Taxes:

If you anticipate to owe a significant amount of tax by the end of the year as a side hustler, you may be obliged to pay quarterly estimated taxes. These quarterly payments help you avoid penalties for late payments.

4. Credits and Deductions:

Side hustlers may take advantage of a variety of tax breaks and credits that can assist in reducing their tax obligations. Deductions for home office expenditures, transportation, and supplies are common.

5. Keeping Records:

It is essential to have accurate and well-organized financial records for tax reasons. Maintain a safe and easily accessible area for all receipts, invoices, and financial papers.

6. Speak with a Tax Professional:

Consider hiring a tax expert or accountant to assist you in navigating the complexity of self-employment taxes, deductions, and credits.

Tax Breaks for Side Hustler

Tax deductions may dramatically lower your taxable income and, as a result, the amount of taxes you owe. Here are some popular tax deductions available to side hustlers:

1. Deduction for Home Office:

You may be qualified for the home office deduction if you utilize a portion of your house only for your side business. You may deduct a percentage of your rent or mortgage, utilities, and other home-related expenditures using this deduction.

2. Vehicle Costs:

You may deduct a percentage of your car expenditures, including petrol, maintenance, insurance, and depreciation if you use your vehicle for business activities.

3. Materials and Equipment:

The cost of goods and equipment directly relevant to your side hustle may be deducted.

Office supplies, software, and other equipment or materials utilized in your job are all included.

4. Marketing and Public Relations:

Marketing and advertising expenses for your side business, such as website hosting, internet advertisements, and promotional materials, are tax deductible.

5. Travel Costs:

When traveling for work, you may deduct expenditures such as transportation, housing, meals, and conference fees.

6. Professional Services:

Fees given to experts for advice and services relevant to your side hustle, such as accountants, attorneys, or consultants, are tax-deductible.

Best Financial Practices for Your Side Hustle

In addition to monitoring your revenue, spending, and taxes, here are some financial best practices to guarantee your side hustle's financial health and growth:

1. Emergency Reserve Fund:

Maintain an emergency reserve to meet unforeseen bills or variations in income. This financial buffer offers security and stability.

2. Retirement Preparation:

Consider creating a side business retirement plan. A Simplified Employee Pension (SEP) IRA or a Solo 401(k) are two options. Retirement planning is critical for your long-term financial well-being.

3. Debt Administration:

If you have company debt, devise a plan to pay it off as quickly as possible. Debt reduction or elimination may liberate resources for investment and development.

4. Financial Check-Ins regularly:

Set up frequent financial check-ins to talk through your income, spending, and financial objectives. These check-ins enable you to make educated financial choices for your side business.

5. Financial Objectives:

Set financial targets for your side venture. Whether it's boosting sales, entering new markets, or introducing a new product,

Chapter 9: Scaling Your Side Hustle

Starting a side hustle is an exciting path that many individuals take on to make additional money, pursue their hobbies, or try out new company ideas. However, many side hustlers' ultimate goal is to grow their companies into full-fledged corporations. This book will walk you through the steps of growing your side hustle, including growth, recruiting, and outsourcing techniques. We'll also share inspirational tales of people who converted their side hustles into great businesses.

The Evolution of a Side Hustle into a Full-Fledged Business

The leap from a side hustle to a full-fledged company requires more than simply expanding your operations; it also requires a considerable adjustment in thinking and dedication. When you're ready to take the plunge, follow these steps to get started:

1. Establish Your Vision:

Begin by outlining your long-term vision. How does your full-fledged company appear? What are your ambitions and goals over the next several years? This vision will be your compass during the scaling process.

2. Determine Market Viability:

Before expanding, be sure there is a market for your goods or services. Conduct extensive market research to verify your company's idea and ensure a sustained consumer base.

3. Lay a Firm Foundation:

Formalize your side hustle to build a strong company basis. Register your company, get the required permits, and establish correct financial and legal structures. This is a critical stage for long-term stability.

4. Financial Management:

Analyze your financial condition and create a scaled budget. Determine the amount of money required to invest in growth and expansion. From marketing and merchandise to more workers and office space, your budget should cover it all.

5. Scaling Techniques:

Implementing tactics that enable you to service more consumers and produce more income is at the heart of growing your side hustle. Consider the following strategies:

Diversification is broadening your product or service offerings to attract a larger client base.

Invest in a strong online presence by developing a professional website, e-commerce capabilities, and social media marketing.

Marketing and Promotion: Expand your marketing efforts to reach a larger audience. Make use of both online and offline channels.

Hiring and Outsourcing: Hire more people or outsource duties to free up time for strategic choices.

Process Optimization: Improve efficiency and production by streamlining your processes.

Customer Service: To maintain current customers and attract new ones, focus on offering exceptional customer service.

6. Building a Team:

Scaling often necessitates the expansion of your workforce. Evaluate your requirements and consider employing workers with complementary talents and experience to your own. Hiring may be a significant investment, so be sure it fits with your growth plan.

7. Strategic Outsourcing:

Outsourcing may be a cost-effective approach to get access to specialized expertise without the long-term commitment that comes with employing people. Consider outsourcing jobs like accounting, graphic design, or marketing to free up your time for vital company operations.

8. Technology and Systems:

Invest in methods and technologies that will help you to run your business more efficiently. To efficiently manage expansion, use customer relationship management (CRM) software, inventory management systems, and e-commerce platforms.

9. Check and Adjust:

Monitor your company's success regularly and alter your plans as appropriate. Scaling is a continual process, and your strategy may need to be fine-tuned in response to market developments, consumer feedback, and internal insights.

10. Seek Funding if Required:

You may need more money depending on the scope of your growth. Loans, grants, venture financing, and even crowdsourcing are all options. Examine your finance requirements carefully and look into the most relevant options.

Inspiring Tales of Side Hustles Turned Businesses

Let's look at the inspirational experiences of people who successfully converted their passion projects into profitable businesses to obtain insight into the process of growing a side hustle.

Case Study 1: The Handmade Soap Maker

Meet Lisa, who began her side business by making homemade soaps. She began by selling her items at local craft festivals and internet markets. Lisa intended to expand her operation into a full-fledged soap-making enterprise as demand expanded.

Scaling Techniques:

Lisa expanded her product range to include a variety of soap fragrances and varieties, such as organic, vegan, and specialty soaps.

She established an online presence by launching a professional e-commerce website where clients could explore and buy her items.

Lisa used social media marketing, email newsletters, and local events to promote her company and attract a larger consumer base.

Hiring and Outsourcing: Lisa employed part-time workers and outsourced packing and shipping to meet production needs.

Systems & Technology: To simplify her operations, she purchased inventory management software and an e-commerce platform.

Lisa's passion for her art, along with deliberate scaling initiatives, enabled her to develop her handmade soap side hustle into a thriving company. She grew her consumer base by expanding her distribution to retail locations.

Case Study 2: The Freelance Writer Who Became the Owner of a Content Agency

Meet Alex, a freelance writer who began his side career by writing for customers on a freelancing website. As his customer base developed, Alex wanted to expand his business and establish a content agency.

Scaling Techniques:

Diversification: The firm added content marketing, copywriting, and social media management to its offerings.

Alex created a professional agency website to highlight the team's talents and portfolio.

Marketing and Promotion: To recruit customers, the firm employed a mix of content marketing, email campaigns, and targeted social media advertising.

Hiring and Outsourcing: To keep up with the agency's rising workload, Alex employed more freelance writers and content producers. He also delegated chores like website design and SEO to specialists.

Systems and Technology: To improve client communication and project tracking, the agency installed project management software.

Alex's transformation from freelance writer to business owner enabled him to take on bigger projects, work with a broad variety of customers, and establish a respected brand in the content marketing sector.

Case 3: The Home-Based Baker Who Became a Bakery Owner

Sarah, an enthusiastic baker, began her side business by selling handmade cakes and cupcakes to friends and family. She decided to launch her bakery as demand for her baked delicacies increased.

Scaling Techniques:

Sarah expanded her bakery's product line to include bread, pastries, and a variety of baked delicacies.

Online Presence: She developed a professional website with an online ordering system for the convenience of her customers.

Sarah used social media marketing to display her gorgeous baked products, partnered with local influencers and participated in community events.

Hiring and Outsourcing: To satisfy the rising demand, Sarah employed more bakers and front-of-house employees.

For efficient operations, the bakery installed point-of-sale systems, inventory management, and digital order tracking.

Sarah's passion for baking and deliberate scaling efforts transformed her home-based side hustle into a profitable bakery company that drew clients from all over the area.

Scaling Difficulties and How to Overcome Them

While growing a side hustle may be very gratifying, it also has its own set of problems. Here are some frequent issues and solutions for dealing with them:

1. Financial Restriction:

Scaling involves substantial expenditure for marketing, recruiting, equipment, and space. Many side hustlers have difficulties in obtaining money.

Consider alternative financing possibilities, such as loans, grants, investors, or profit reinvestment. Assess your budget carefully and prioritize your expenditures.

2. Time Administration:

Balancing your full-time employment, personal life, and growing initiatives may be difficult.

Solution: Assign tasks, hire staff or freelancers, and create a work plan. Time management is essential for success.

3. Risk Control:

Scaling has inherent risks, such as possible financial losses or market changes.

Conduct rigorous risk assessments and create contingency strategies. Keep an eye on your financial situation and be ready for any surprises.

4. Operational Effectiveness:

Maintaining operational efficiency as your side business increases might be a challenge.

Invest in technology and systems that simplify operations as a solution. Evaluate and improve your processes regularly.

5. Keeping Quality:

Maintaining the quality of your goods or services is critical as you grow.

Solution: Make certain that quality control mechanisms are in place and that they are regularly maintained. It is critical to train and hire the proper people.

6. Retention of Customers:

The difficulty is that scaling may often lead to the neglect of current clients, reducing customer loyalty.

Implement a solid customer relationship management approach. Thank your loyal customers and continue to give outstanding service.

Last Thoughts

The path from side hustle to full-fledged enterprise is a tribute to hard work, perseverance, and intelligent decision-making. While difficulties are unavoidable, they may be handled with careful preparation, investment, and a willingness to adapt. Keep your long-term goal in mind as you expand your side hustle, and remember that the sky is the limit when it comes to converting your passion or concept into a profitable company. The journey may be difficult, but the benefits are well worth the effort.

Chapter 10: Overcoming Challenges and Staying Motivated

Running a side business is a wonderful adventure full of potential for personal development and financial benefit. However, like with any business effort, it is not without its difficulties. In this chapter, we'll look at some of the most typical challenges that side hustlers face and provide solutions to solve them. We'll also provide advice on how to remain motivated and persistent throughout your side hustle adventure. Finally, we'll go through the necessity of finding mentorship and networking to move your side hustle ahead.

Common Obstacles that Side Hustlers Face

Time Management: Juggling a side business with full-time work and a personal life may be difficult. Finding time for your side job while still fulfilling your other obligations might be difficult.

Financial constraints: Many side hustlers start with little amounts of money, making it difficult to invest in growth, marketing, or necessary equipment and resources.

Market Competition: Depending on your niche, you may be up against tough competition. It might be difficult to break through the noise and distinguish oneself.

Burnout: Juggling several obligations and working long hours may lead to burnout, affecting both your full-time job and your side business.

Isolation: Side hustlers often work alone, which may be lonely. Motivation may be impacted by a lack of teamwork and the absence of coworkers.

Regulatory and Tax Issues: It may be difficult to navigate the complicated world of self-employment taxes and company laws.

Strategies for Overcoming Obstacles

Time Administration:

Tasks should be prioritized: Identify and prioritize the most crucial activities that will propel your side hustle ahead.

Establish boundaries: To avoid burnout, set clear limits for your side hustle business and personal life.

Make a schedule: Plan your week ahead of time, devoting particular time blocks to your side hustle activities.

Financial Restriction:

Bootstrapping is starting with what you have and progressively reinvesting revenues into your firm to generate development.

Investigate low-cost marketing: Make use of no-cost or low-cost marketing tactics such as content marketing, social media, and email campaigns.

Seek financial assistance: To overcome early financial constraints, consider small company loans, crowdsourcing, or grants.

Market Competence:

Focus on a unique niche within your sector that may have less competition, enabling you to stand out.

Make your brand stand out: Emphasize what distinguishes your side hustle, whether it's your strategy, quality, or customer service.

Learning that is ongoing: To surpass competition, stay current on industry developments and always enhance your abilities.

Burnout:

Delegate or outsource tasks: To lessen your burden, delegate or outsource specific jobs to freelancers or virtual assistants.

Take frequent breaks: Plan small pauses throughout the day to refuel and prevent burnout.

To maintain a good work-life balance, prioritize self-care activities such as exercise, meditation, or hobbies.

Isolation:

Participate in a group: To connect with like-minded people, look for online or local clubs, forums, or networking events connected to your business or side hustle.

Collaborate: Consider working on projects with other side hustlers to create a feeling of camaraderie and shared goals.

Regulatory and Tax Issues:

Speak with a professional: Seek advice from a tax professional or accountant who has worked with self-employed persons.

Maintain your organization: Keep detailed records of your income, spending, and financial activities to simplify tax filing.

Maintaining Motivation and Persistence

Motivation and perseverance are essential for your side hustle's long-term success. Here are some methods to help you keep your excitement and remain on track:

Set explicit, quantifiable, and Achievable objectives: Set explicit, quantifiable, and attainable objectives for your side business. Having a clear vision and goals can help you stay focused and motivated.

Recognize and appreciate even the smallest accomplishments and milestones. This positive reinforcement might help you stay motivated.

Imagine Success: Make a vision board or frequently imagine your objectives and how you will achieve them. Visualization may motivate you to persevere.

Divide Large jobs into Smaller Steps: Large jobs might be intimidating. Divide them into smaller, more manageable stages to make success seem more attainable.

Keep educated and motivated: To keep educated and motivated, read books, listen to podcasts, or follow thought leaders in your area. Learning from the experiences of others might rekindle your drive.

Connect with Mentors: Seek advice and direction from experienced mentors who may provide insights and support. Their advice may assist you in overcoming obstacles and remaining motivated.

The Value of Seeking Help and Networking

Support and networking are vital resources for side hustlers wanting to expand their businesses. Here's why they're necessary:

Mentors and advisors: Mentors offer expertise and insight to the table, assisting you in navigating problems and making sound judgments. They may give advice, wisdom, and encouragement when it is required.

Opportunities for Networking: Connecting with individuals in your business or who have similar interests may lead to new opportunities, partnerships, and collaborations. Networking may also introduce you to new viewpoints and thoughts.

Emotional Support: Running a side hustle may be an emotional rollercoaster, with highs of achievement and lows of disappointments. A support network may offer the emotional support required to persist.

Accountability may be achieved by sharing your objectives and progress with others. Knowing that others are aware of your goals might help you keep on track.

To use the power of collaboration and networking:

Attend industry events, conferences, and seminars to network with other professionals.

Join relevant online forums, social media groups, or networking platforms.

Look for networking events or gatherings in your area or online.

Approach prospective mentors or advisers with a specific request for mentoring or advice.

Join mastermind groups or business alliances to share your thoughts and experiences.

Conclusion

Running a side business is a unique venture with its own set of problems and hurdles. You can overcome these obstacles and reach your side hustle objectives with the correct techniques, motivation, and support. You'll be well-equipped to traverse the side hustle environment and turn your enterprise into a flourishing success if you manage your time, funds, and taxes well, remain motivated and tenacious, and seek out mentors and networking opportunities. Remember that although the trip may be difficult, the benefits are well worth the effort.

www.ingramcontent.com/pod-product-compliance
Lightning Source LLC
Chambersburg PA
CBHW072213290526
45794CB00004B/1744